THE REASON
WHY

is Christianity credible?
is there a God?
does man need Him?
is the Bible true?
is man responsible to God?
can man find Divine forgiveness?

when honest with himself,
man questions his existence,
he wonders at his world—
it's beginning and end
he searches for personal meaning

this man has explored life
and found its fulfillment
here he explains the
intellectual evidence he weighed
the questions he had answered
the resulting belief he experienced

Robert Laidlaw is convinced of God's reality
he believes in the Bible
in Christ
in Divine salvation
in purposeful living
in credible Christianity

THE REASON WHY

By Robert A. Laidlaw

Lamplighter Books Grand Rapids, Michigan
Zondervan Publishing House

THE REASON WHY
First Zondervan printing 1970

Lamplighter Books are published by Zondervan
Publishing House, 1415 Lake Drive, S.E.
Grand Rapids, Michigan 49506

ISBN 0-310-27112-6

Printed in the United States of America

90 91 92 93 94 / LP / 30 29 28 27 26

The Reason Why

Written by a Christian businessman to the members of his staff...

SUPPOSE that a young man sent his fiancee a diamond ring costing him $1000, placing it in a little case which the jeweller threw in for nothing. How disappointed he would be, if upon meeting her a few days later, she would say, "Sweetheart, that was a lovely little box you sent me. To take special care of it, I promise to keep it wrapped up in a safe place so that no harm shall come to it."

Rather ridiculous, isn't it? Yet it is just as foolish for men and women to be spending all their time and thought on their bodies, which are only cases containing the real self, the soul, which, the Bible tells us, will persist long after our bodies have crumbled to dust. The soul is of infinite value. Longfellow expressed it this way:

> Tell me not in mournful numbers,
>   Life is but an empty dream,
> For the soul is dead that slumbers,
>   And things are not what they seem.
>
> Life is real, life is earnest,
>   And the grave is not its goal.
> Dust thou art, to dust returnest,
>   Was not spoken of the soul.

Indeed this statement was not made of the soul, for in Mark 8:36 our Lord Himself asks, "What shall it profit a man if he gain the whole world and lose his own soul?" So, in Christ's estimate, man's soul is something incomparably more valuable than the whole world.

I would like to discuss with you some of the basic things that relate to your most valuable possession, your soul. For instance —

> Is there a God?
> Is the Bible true?
> Is man accountable?
> Is there divine forgiveness?

These are some of the problems which most perplex those who think seriously about the future.

How may I know there is a God?

I have an innate conviction that God exists. No matter how my intellect has tried, in the past, to produce reasons proving He was not, or how much I have wanted to believe that there was no God, that "still, small voice" came to me again and again, just as it has come to you, in the quiet of life's more sober moments. Yes, I knew that at least for me there was a God. And as I looked at others I realized how many were looking for God, seeking in "religion" to silence that same voice that spoke within me.

True, there are some men who don't
6 believe in God. But to me the problems

of unbelief in God are greater than the problems of belief. To believe that unaided dead matter produced life, that living matter produced mind, that mind produced conscience, and that the chaos of chance produced the cosmos of order as we see it in nature, seems to call not for faith but for credulity.

The president of the New York Scientific Society once gave eight reasons why he believed there was a God. The first was this: Take ten identical coins and mark them one to ten. Place them in your pocket. Now take one out. There is one chance in ten that you will get number one. Now replace it, and the chances that number two will follow number one are not one in ten, but one in one hundred. With each new coin taken out, the risk will be multiplied by ten, so that the chance of ten following nine is one in 10,000,000,000 (ten billion). It seemed so unbelievable to me that I immediately took pencil and paper and very quickly discovered he was right. Try it yourself.

That is why George Gallup, the American statistician says: "I could prove God statistically. Take the human body alone — the chance that all its functions would just happen is a statistical monstrosity."

Surely no thoughtful persons would wish to base their eternal future on a "statistical monstrosity." Perhaps that is why the Bible says in Psalm 14:1: "The fool hath said in his heart there is no

God." But let us consider the problem from another viewpoint.

Suppose we are standing at an airport watching a big jet come in for a landing. I say to you, "A lot of people think that plane is the result of someone's carefully designed plans, but I know better. There was really no intelligence at work on it at all. In some strange way the metal just came out of the ground, and fashioned itself into flat sheets. And then these metal sheets slowly began to grow together and formed the body and wings and tail. Then after a long while the engines slowly grew in place, and one day some people came along and discovered the plane, all finished and ready to fly."

You would probably consider me a lunatic and move further into the crowd to escape my senseless chatter. Why? You know that where there is a design there must be a designer, and having seen other productions of the human mind just like the plane in question, you are positive that it was planned by human intelligence and built by human skill.

Yet there are highly educated, professional men who tell us that the entire universe came into being by chance, that there was really no higher intelligence at work on it. They claim to know no God but nature.

On the other hand there are many thoughtful men who believe that God is transcendent; that is, while He reveals Himself in nature (in that its laws and principles are expressions of His power and wisdom), He Himself is greater than the universe. But all that atheists can offer us is the riddle of design without a designer, of creation without a Creator, of effect without cause.

Every thoughtful person believes in a series of causes and effects in nature, each effect becoming the cause of some other effect. The acceptance of this as fact logically compels one to admit that there must be a beginning to any series. There could never have been a first effect if there had not been a First Cause. This First Cause to me is Deity.

Although man has discovered many of the laws that govern electricity, the greatest scientists cannot really define it. Then why do we believe it exists? Because we see the manifestation of its existence in our homes and industries and streets. Though I do not know where God came from, I must believe He exists, because I see the manifestations of Him everywhere around me.

Dr. Wernher von Braun, director of NASA research, and developer of the rocket which put America's first space satellite into orbit says:

"In our modern world, many people seem to feel that our rapid advances in the field of science render such things as religious belief untimely or old-fashioned. They wonder why we should be satisfied in 'believing' something when science tells us that we 'know' so many things. The simple answer to this contention is that we are confronted with many more mysteries of nature today than when the age of scientific enlightenment began. With every new answer unfolded, science has consistently discovered at least three new questions.

"The answers indicate that anything as well ordered and perfectly created as is our earth and universe must have a Maker, a Master Designer. Anything so orderly, so perfect, so precisely balanced, so majestic as this creation can only be the product of a Divine idea."

The late professor Edwin Conklin, a noted biologist, very aptly said: "The probability of life originating from accident is comparable to the probability of an Unabridged Dictionary resulting from an explosion in a printing shop."

God exists whether or not men may choose to believe in Him. The reason why many people do not believe in God is not so much that it is intellectually impossible to believe in God but because belief in God forces the thoughtful person to face the fact that he is accountable to such a God. Many people are unwilling to do this. Most of those who take refuge in atheism or agnosticism do so because it is a convenient "escape" from the stern reality that man is accountable to his Creator. It is usually not so much a case of "I cannot believe" as it is a case of "I do not want to believe."

I know only two ways by which God's purpose and God's person may be known. First there is the process of reason. As a good detective can, for example, tell you many things about my skills, habits and character just by examining something I may have made or handled, so much can be learned about God by a careful examination of the universe, the work of His hands.

But the detective who examines only what I make can never say that he knows *me*. He may know some things about me, but before he can say that he knows me, there must be a process of revelation: I must communicate with him. I must tell him what I think, how I feel and what I want to do. This self-revelation may be in conversation, in writing, or in some other way. Only then does it become possible for him to know me. Just so, if God is ever to be known and His thoughts, desires and purposes perceived, He must take the initiative and make at least a partial revelation of Himself to men.

Of all the many books this world contains there is one only that claims to be a direct revelation from God, telling us of Himself and His purposes for us. That book is the Bible. The Bible is a book of such importance that it is surely worthy of thoughtful investigation. So, with the advice of Francis Bacon neither to accept nor reject, but to weigh and consider, let us approach this book with its unusual claims.

To be fair to ourselves and to the Bible, we should read it through. As a judge must not make his decision when the case is half heard, neither must we. Rather, like the judge, we should compare the evidence of the witnesses, and weigh and consider every word, seeking for its deepest significance rather than accepting its surface meaning. Surely the importance of its claims justifies spending the necessary time, on the study of its sixty-six books, written by at least forty different writers (some well educated, some barely educated, some kings, some peasants) over a period of 1600 years in places as far apart as Babylon in Asia and Rome in Europe. With such authorship one would expect to find a miscellaneous collection of contradictory statements. Its unity is therefore especially striking, for each contribution is the complement of the others.

In my considerations of this whole matter, slowly the truth of 2 Peter 1:21 became certain to me. There was no other reasonable explanation. "Holy men of God spoke as they were moved by the Holy Ghost." This belief was confirmed as I read prophecy after prophecy in the Old Testament which found its fulfillment, even to the letter, hundreds of years later. For instance, Isaiah 53 foretold the death of Christ with minute accuracy more than 700 years before His crucifixion. Yes, the difficulties in the way of doubting the Book seemed to me greater than those in the way of believing it. I had to be honest with myself and admit that the problems were all on the side of unbelief. I even went further and said:

"I believe the Bible to be the word of the living God. I can account for it in no other way."

Such an admission brought me face to face with a serious difficulty, however, for the Bible set a standard of righteousness that I had not attained. It pronounced that anything short of its standard was sin. Remembering that God knows your every secret thought, just measure yourself alongside the standard: "Thou shalt love the Lord thy God with *all* thy heart, and with *all* thy soul, and with *all* thy mind. This is the first and great commandment" (Matthew 22:37, 38).

Confronted with such a standard, can you claim to have lived up to it throughout your life? Have you put God first in everything? No man can honestly claim such perfection. Every honest heart echoes Romans 3:10 and 23: "There is none righteous, no, not one. . . . All have sinned, and come short of the glory of

God." All have failed to reach God's standard.

A young man once asked me, "Do you think it fair of God to set the standard of holiness so high that we cannot reach it, and then judge us for falling short?"

I replied, "God has not set an arbitrary standard of holiness as an official sets an arbitrary standard of height for his bodyguards. In such a case, a man may have all the other qualifications, but if he is an inch too short he is disqualified.

"God has not really set a standard at all; He is the standard. He is absolute holiness, and to preserve His own character He must remain absolutely holy in all of His dealings with man, maintaining that standard irrespective of the tremendous implications which it may hold for both Him and us."

My conscience and my common sense compelled me to admit I had fallen short of God's standard of absolute holiness and, therefore, I was a sinner in His sight.

On my admission of having sinned came God's condemnation in Ezekiel 18:4: "The soul that sinneth, it shall die."

It appealed to me like this: The law in Great Britain says that all drivers must keep to the left side of the street, while in New York the rule of the road demands that a driver keep to the right side. Now, suppose I go driving in London and keep to the right side. On being 14 brought before the judge, I say, "This is ridiculous. In the United States we are allowed to drive on the right side."

"You are not being judged by the laws of America," he replies. "It does not matter what the laws of other lands may be, you should have concerned yourself only with the laws which judge you here, where you are."

In the same way as far as God's standard was concerned, I was lost, because God's standard was the only one by which I was to be judged in eternity. I was hopelessly lost. I began to see that it didn't matter at all what I thought, or what my friends told me. The judgment would be on what God has said, not what my friends say. Moreover, because in God's judgment we had all sinned, there was no use in looking to other men for help, for they were under the same condemnation as I.

But this same Bible, which told me of my sin, told me also of Jesus Christ, who claimed to be the Son of God.

It is the clear teaching of the Bible that this person, Jesus Christ, is God the Son. He saw that men were lost and that they had forfeited their lives to sin. His life was not forfeited. It was sinless and spotless. This pure life of His He was willing to give in place of man's sinful life, that we might go free.

He Himself tells us in John 3:16 that "God so loved the world, that he gave his only begotten Son, that whosoever believeth in him should not perish, but have everlasting life."

If Jesus Christ is the Son of God, then we may indeed be sure of salvation; but the difficulty faces us: Is Jesus Christ really the Son of God? He could only be one of three — the Son of God, or a deceiver, or an honest man Himself under a hallucination. But we find Him meeting some of the cleverest men of His day, who were purposely sent to catch Him in His words, and He so silenced them that they did not dare ask Him any more questions (Matthew 22:46). And when we ourselves consider the wisdom of His statements from an intellectual standpoint, we see plainly that He was under no hallucination as to Himself.

Then was His wisdom so great that He was using it to deceive the people? Have you ever heard of a young man associating with swindlers and rogues and because of that association becoming ennobled, pure and honest? No! You admit you have not heard of such a case; but I know a young man who by the reception of Christ into his life has been lifted from the basest desires to the noblest manhood. I simply cannot believe that the reception of a deceiver into one's life could transform it for good.

The other day I heard a man say, "I owe it to Jesus Christ that I can walk down the street with my head held erect and my shoulders squared to the world.

I owe it to Him that I can look a pure woman in the face and grip an honest man by the hand."

I call to witness the opinion of the whole civilized world that Jesus Christ was at least a good man. If so, then an honest man, and if honest He must have been what He claimed to be, the Son of God, sent to lay down His sinless life in place of your sinful life and mine.

Leaders from several professions have this to say about Jesus Christ:

United States Senator Mark O. Hatfield, testifies: "I saw that for 31 years I had lived for self and decided I wanted to live the rest of my life only for Jesus Christ. I asked God to forgive my self-centered life and to make my life His own. Following Jesus Christ has been an experience of increasing challenge, adventure and happiness. Living a committed Christian life is truly satisfying because it has given me true purpose and direction by serving not myself, but Jesus Christ."

Robert E. (Bob) Richards, former Olympic track star, said: "My only reason for being in sports is to give my testimony to youth of all the world that Jesus Christ can save from sin, and that one can be a Christian and still excel in good, creative things. Young people need to realize that God unleashed a tremendous spiritual power when Jesus Christ died on Calvary."

Lt. Gen. William K. Harrison (Ret.), former Senior Delegate of the United Nations Command Truce Team in Korea and later Commander-in-Chief of the Caribbean Command, wrote: "It is wonderful to believe in the Lord Jesus Christ and I am exceedingly thankful that God has graciously led me to saving faith in Christ. God gives us who believe in Christ a daily, personal experience which is convincing evidence of the reality of the new life in Christ."

Convinced that the Scripture is true, that Jesus Christ is the Son of God, believing that He willingly came, that God so loved me that He has willingly sent Him to suffer the full penalty of my sins that I might go free, if I would retain my self-respect as an intelligent being, I must accept the Lord Jesus Christ as my Saviour.

But I do not ask you to accept Him as yours, for you may have an objection: although it is plausible that the Bible is true, are not alternate views also plausible? Why not be reasonable and submit them to a fair test as well?

On telling my conviction to a friend, he replied, "You are all right, but so am I, although I don't see things as you do. It seems to me that it doesn't matter so much what a man believes, so long as he is sincere in his belief."

Let us test that statement. One fine Sunday morning a neighbor of mine said to his wife and family, "Let us take the car and go for a picnic." Traveling north, he came to a railway crossing and, sincerely believing there would be no trains on a Sunday morning, attempted to drive across. He was killed on the spot, one son had an arm broken and his little daughter was in a cast for months. Did his sincere belief that all was clear save him? No, it did not.

I know a nurse who, on night duty, sincerely believed she held the right medicine in her hand, but she was wrong, and in twenty minutes her patient was dead in spite of frantic efforts to save him.

Of course we need sincerity, but we must sincerely believe truth, not error. In fact, having sincere belief in error can be the very means of deceiving and finally destroying us.

The Bible leaves no room for doubt. In John 14:6 Christ says: "I am the way, the truth and the life; *no man cometh unto the Father but by me.*" Acts 4:12 states: "There is *no other name* under heaven given among men whereby we must be saved." If you can get to heaven any other way you will be a witness throughout eternity to the fact that Jesus Christ spoke falsely when He said there was *no other way.* But, since He gives full evidence of being the Son of God, is it not folly to attempt coming to God by any other way than through Christ Himself, who claims to be God's appointed way?

The real reason we want some other way is because the way of the cross is a humbling way and we are proud at heart. But let us remember the way of the cross was a humbling way for Christ also, as we read in Philippians 2:5-8:

5 Have this attitude in yourselves which was also in Christ Jesus,

6 Who, although He existed in the form of God, did not regard equality with God a thing to be grasped,

7 But emptied Himself, taking the form of a bondservant and being made in the likeness of men.

8 And being found in appearance as a man, He humbled Himself by becoming obedient to the point of death, even death on a cross. (*The New American Standard Bible — New Testament*)

Some people have suggested that all a person needs to do is sincerely reform, do better in the future, and thus live down past short-comings. This is supposed to make one fit for heaven. Will this work?

Let us assume that the manager of a business goes to his accountant and finds that his company owes $50,000 to manufacturers and other merchants. He says, "Write letters to all those people and tell

20

them that we are not going to trouble about the past, that we have turned over new pages in our ledger, but we promise to pay 100 cents on the dollar in all future business, and from now on live up to the highest standard of business integrity." The accountant would think his employer had gone mad, and would refuse to put such a proposition to the creditors. Yet thousands of otherwise sensible people are trying to get to heaven by just such a proposal, offering to meet their obligations toward God for the future, but refusing to worry about the past at all. Yet in Ecclesiastes 3:15 we read, "God requireth that which is past." Even if we assume that we can somehow begin to live an absolutely perfect life — which is no better than we ought to do, but which is certainly impossible for us — we are still sinners.

God's righteousness demands that no past account shall be considered settled till it has been paid to the last penny and every claim of justice met. The murderer may cover his sin and live the life of a model citizen for ten years after his crime, but when he is discovered, man's law condemns him to death. Though he has murdered no one for ten long years — it judges him still a murderer.

To hide past sin, either *thoughts, words or deeds,* by what seems to be an absolutely perfect life, still leaves us sinners in the sight of Him to whom the past and future are as open as the present. According to God's standards of holiness, we all have sinned, and *we* must bring that sin out into the open and have it dealt with righteously.

We each need someone who can clear the books. The Bible declares that Jesus Christ is the only One who could pay this penalty. "We were reconciled to God by the death of his Son" (Romans 5:10). Yes, the Lord Jesus Christ gave up His life in place of ours that we might go free. Our past sin is paid for, and God, against whom we had sinned, has given us His receipt showing His satisfaction with the completed work of Christ on the cross in that He raised Him from the dead. Christ once crucified is now our living Saviour. He died to save us from the penalty of sin and now He lives to deliver us from the power of sin.

But why did Christ need to die? Could He not have saved us without that? Man had broken God's law and the penalty was death. How could Christ righteously deliver us without meeting our full penalty? Do you not see that if He paid anything less than the full price there would still be judgment for us to meet? But it is evident that because He died, the law we had broken can judge us no more.

The Bible says in Romans 8:1: "There is therefore now no condemnation to them which are in Christ Jesus."

22   On one occasion an unfinished court

case extended to a second day and as is the usual practice, so that no outside influence could be brought to bear on the jurymen, they were kept in custody overnight. On entering the court the next morning the Judge, addressing the jury, said: "Gentlemen, the case is dismissed; the prisoner has been called to a higher court." The accused had died in his cell during the night and there was no use going on with the case, since the law cannot judge a dead man.

Again, if a man should murder one person he is put to death, but if he should murder six people he is still just put to death, because this is the *utmost penalty* of the law. No matter what a man's sins may be, the law knows no greater penalty than to take his life.

Therefore it matters not though there are sins in my life that I have long since forgotten. I fear none of them, for I have this confidence that the Lord Jesus Christ, my Substitute, suffered the *utmost penalty of the law* on my account, freeing me absolutely from all its claims against me, both great and small.

On the basis of the greatness of Jesus Christ's sacrifice, *some have suggested that if Christ died for all, we must all be saved*. But God does not say so. He says there is salvation for all, not that all are saved.

Here is an illustration. It is a bitterly cold winter and unemployment is rife in one of our great cities with many in dire need. The municipal authorities provide free meals. You meet a poor fellow on the street who says he is starving. Naturally you ask if he does not believe the notices that are up all over the city, that there is enough food for all provided free.

"Yes," he replies, "I believe that is true in a general sort of way, but I am still hungry."

You tell him that he is likely to remain hungry in spite of the provisions unless he eats and drinks personally of what is provided for all.

Just so, although the death of Christ provides salvation for whosoever will, only those are saved who personally accept Christ and believe that He died in their place. I must take Christ as *my* Saviour, or His death will avail me nothing — just as a man could die of thirst beside a spring of water if he refused to make its life-giving stream his own by drinking of it for himself.

There are some people who still pose the question: How could the Lord Jesus Christ's one life be considered the substitute for the lives of so many, so that God offers salvation to whosoever places their faith in Christ?

That seems a fair question — a problem in arithmetic that can be demonstrated on paper. Christ was God manifest in the flesh — Divinity in humanity

24

— so that the life He gave was an infinite life, which can meet the needs of any number of finite lives. Get a sheet of paper and write down all the big figures you can think of — millions or more — add them up. Now you have a big number, then multiply it by 10 — 100 — by a million if you like — cover sheets of paper and after all you still have a finite number — a number that has bounds set about it — a beginning and an end, however far it may extend. No, by adding finite things together no man has ever been able to make that which is infinite. The *infinite life* of Christ given for sinners is more than sufficient to save all who accept Him as the One who died for them.

But how could Christ suffer for my sins when they were not committed till more than 1900 years after He died? At first this seems a problem to a thoughtful person, but the more thoughtful you are, the more readily you will see the solution. God is omniscient (that is, He knows all things), and God is eternal. In Exodus 3:14 God calls himself "I AM" (present tense), and Christ says in John 8:58: "Before Abraham was, I AM" (present tense). In other words, to one who knows all things and is eternal, there is, as it were, neither past nor future, but one eternal present. Events yet to take place 2000 years ahead must be as clear to Him as events which happened 2000 years ago, and both must of necessity be just as clear to God as events happening now.

But why did not God make man incapable of disobeying His will and therefore incapable of sinning? Such a question is like asking why does not God draw a crooked straight line or a round square, or make an object black all over and white all over at one and the same time. Man is a creature with the power of intelligent choice, so that the question really is: Why didn't God make a creature with the power of intelligent choice and yet without the power of intelligent choice at one and the same time?

If I had the power of hypnotism, I would be able to put my two sons into an hypnotic state, thus robbing them of the power of intelligent choice, and then say, "Sit on those chairs till I return" — "Get up and eat" — "Stop eating" — "Kiss me good night," and unfeeling arms would go around my neck, and unresponsive lips would be pressed to mine. I would have prompt and perfect obedience to my every command, but would I find satisfaction in it? No!

I want boys with free wills who are capable of disobeying me, but who willingly choose to carry out my instructions, which are the outcome of my love for them and are given for their own good. I cannot conceive of God, who put these desires in my heart and yours, being satisfied with anything less Himself.

God does not want puppets who jump in a given direction according to the wire that is pulled, nor does He want robots in the form of "men" who mechanically and absolutely obey His will as do the planets that whirl through space. God can find satisfaction in nothing less than the spontaneous love of our hearts and our free-will decisions to walk in paths that please and honor Him. But it is obvious that this same power of free action enables us to defy and dishonor Him if we so choose.

Man is truly a magnificent creature, far above the animal creation around him. There is no "missing link." But a great gulf is fixed between the highest beast and man, for God has given man the awesome power of being able to say *no* to God as well as an effective *yes*. In your own interests, may I ask which you are saying to God now as you read this booklet?

What Does God Care About This Little World of Ours Compared With the Vastness of the Mighty Universe?

Think of our own solar system, with the planet Neptune thirty times as far away from the sun as our earth, so that it takes 164 of our years to make one of Neptune's, and beyond this, suns with planets revolving around them as our solar system revolves around the sun! 27

Of what importance can our earth be to God, and of how much less importance can man be?

So said the astronomer as the faith of his youth fled — this is what the telescope had done for him. The vastness of the heavens had robbed him of faith in his mother's God, for how could God trouble Himself about man, who is less than a grain of sand in comparison?

But his thirst for knowledge would not let him rest. The heavens were available for study only at night; how should the free hours of the day be spent? Why not a microscope? And lo! worlds were opened at his feet — worlds as wonderful as those above, and slowly his faith came back. Yes, the God who could attend to such minute details as to make a drop of ditch water throb with miniature life was sure to be interested in man, the highest form of His creation. The man found balance instead of bias, and balance brought him back to God. John 3:16 was true after all.

But is faith logical? Yes, it is logical. It is a mistake to think that faith is opposed to reason. Faith and reason go hand in hand, but faith goes on when reason can go no farther. Reason, to a great extent, is dependent on faith, for without knowledge it is impossible to reason, and knowledge is very largely a matter of faith in human testimony. For instance, I believe strychnine administered in a large enough dose will poison a human being, but I have never seen the experiment performed. Yet I have such faith in the written testimony of men that I would not take a large dose of strychnine for anything.

If you check up carefully, you will find that nine-tenths of the things you know (?) are a matter of faith in human testimony, written or spoken, for you have not verified them for yourself. Then, having accepted the testimony of men on other matters, will you not accept the testimony of thousands of Christians when they affirm that they have verified the things written in God's Word and have proved them to be true?

But why should God judge my sins as worthy of death? I cannot answer that, but I would suggest that because of His infinite holiness no sin could exist in His presence. In some primitive cultures a native chief may club his wife to death on slight provocation without falling in the slightest degree in the estimation of his people. The same act in our land would have to be paid for by the life of the murderer. The act is the same in both lands, but in one instance no judgment; in the other, quick retribution. The difference is simply the result of our enlightenment. If a sin, which in a primitive culture is considered as nothing, would cause a man to lose his life in our land, think, if you can, what some other sin, which appears to us as nothing, must look like to an infinitely Holy God — "For God is light, and in him is no darkness at all" (I John 1:5).

It may be just, but is it merciful of God to refuse to take us all to heaven even if we reject Christ as our sin-bearer? Yes, both just and merciful. Would it be kindness to transfer a poor ragged beggar into the glare of a beautiful ballroom? Would he not be more conscious of his rags and dirt? Would he not do his best to escape again to the darkness of the street? He would be infinitely happier there. Would it be kindness and mercy on God's part to bring a man in his sins into the holy light of Heaven if that man had rejected God's offer of the only cleansing power there is? If you and I would not wish our friends to see inside our minds now and read all the thoughts that have ever been there (and our friends' standards are perhaps not any higher than our own), what would it be like to stand before God, whose absolute holiness would reveal our sin in all its awfulness?

Revelation 6:16 tells us of the feelings of those who refuse to accept Jesus Christ as their Saviour and persist in going to eternity in their sins. They call on the mountains and the rocks to fall on them and hide them from the face of Him that sitteth on the throne. Yet it is the presence of this same Christ that will make Heaven for those who have accepted Him as Saviour and Lord.

You see the absurdity of talking about God taking us all to heaven — heaven is a condition as well as a place. The presence of the Lord Jesus Christ will constitute heaven to those who are cleansed from their sins, while that same presence would make a hell of remorse in the hearts of any who, still in their sins, should stand in the infinite light of His holiness. Let us be quite reasonable — could you really be happy in the presence of One whose love you had rejected, and whose great sacrifice you had not counted worthy of your acceptance?

Salvation by Substitution
or
The Innocent Bearing the Penalty for the Guilty

We have considered reasonable evidence that God does exist and that He has revealed in the Bible His holy claims on men and women. We have been shown that "all have sinned, and come short of the glory of God" (Romans 3:23). We have been faced with Jesus Christ, God's Son, who came to this earth to die for the sin of man. We have also considered numerous objections raised by people who have other ideas about God's plan of salvation. Now we are going to think through the wisdom and the wonder of God's plan of salvation for sinful people. In a word, it is salvation by substitution.

God's love would have forgiven the sinner, but God's righteousness prevented the forgiveness. God's righteousness would have judged the sinner, but God's love restrained the judgment. How to reconcile His inherent righteousness with His character of essential love was a problem that no human philosopher could have solved, but divine wisdom and mercy find their highest expression in the solution — the vicarious suffering and death of God the Son.

"But," one may object, "does not Christianity fail at its very foundation by basing everything on substitution? Substitution will not stand thoughtful investigation. It makes Christ, the Innocent, bear the penalty for the guilty and thus lets the guilty go free. It is diametrically opposed to our every idea of justice, for we believe that justice should protect the innocent and bring the full penalty upon the guilty."

But see God's perfect justice and perfect mercy revealed at the cross. He does not there take the innocent and compel him to bear the penalty of the guilty. God acts like the judge in this story: — It is on record that of two young men who studied law together, one rose to a seat on the bench, while the other took to drink and wasted his life. On one occasion this poor fellow was brought before his old companion, charged with crime, and the lawyers present wondered what kind of justice would be administered by the judge under such trying circumstances. To their surprise, he sentenced his one-time companion to the heaviest penalty the law allowed, and then paid the fine himself and set his old friend free.

God, against whom we had sinned, in justice sat upon His judgment throne and passed the heaviest penalty He could — the sentence of death upon the sinner. Then, in mercy, He stepped down from His throne and in the person of His Son took the sinner's place, bearing the full penalty Himself, for 2 Corinthians 5:19 tells us "that God was *in* Christ," not *through* Christ, but *in* Christ, "reconciling the world unto himself."

God the Father, God the Son, and God the Holy Spirit are one God. The same God against whom we had sinned passed the judgment, paid the penalty, and now offers us full and free pardon, based upon absolute righteousness. That is why the Apostle Paul writes in Romans 1:16, 17: "I am not ashamed of the gospel of Christ, for it is the power of God unto salvation to everyone that believeth ... for therein is the righteousness of God revealed...." I, too, can say I am not ashamed of the Gospel of Christ, for no man can honestly find a flaw in the righteous forgiveness offered by God to man. That is the righteousness you may possess now, at this very moment, if you will accept it.

But is the acceptance of Christ as my Saviour *all* that is necessary to save me for all eternity? Yes. I admit the very simplicity of it seems to make it hard to grasp. But if I owe $500 and have nothing with which to pay, and a friend pays the debt for me and gives me the receipt, I don't worry about it any more. I can look my creditor straight in the face, for I hold his signed receipt. As Jesus Christ gave His life in place of mine, He said: "It is finished," meaning that the work of atonement was completed, and God gave me His receipt. The assurance that He was satisfied with Christ's finished work is that He (God) raised Christ from the dead on the third day.

"But I can't see it," said a certain cabinetmaker, as a friend tried to explain this to him. At last an idea came to his friend, who, lifting a plane, made as though he would plane the top of a beautifully polished table that stood near.

"Stop!" cried the cabinetmaker. "Don't you see that's finished? You'll simply ruin it if you use that plane on it."

"Why," replied his friend, "that's just what I have been trying to show you about Christ's work of redemption. It was finished when He gave His life for you, and if you try to add to that finished work you can only spoil it. Just accept it as it stands — His life for yours, and you go free." Like a flash the cabinetmaker saw it and received Jesus Christ into his life as his Saviour.

"But," says someone, "there is one more problem that puzzles me. I know a polished cultured gentleman who is not a Christian and states so quite definitely, and I know a rather crude uncultured man who is a Christian and who shows his genuine belief in many ways. Do you mean to tell me God prefers the uncultured man simply because he has accepted and acknowledged Christ as his Saviour?" This question arises from a confusion of ideas. A Christian is not different in degree from a non-Christian, he is different in *kind*, just as the difference between a diamond and a cabbage is not one of degree, but of kind. The one is polished, the other is crude, but the one is dead while the other is alive, therefore the one has what the other has not in any degree whatever, *life* — and such is the difference God sees between a Christian and a non-Christian.

Here is one of many such statements He makes in His Word. I John 5:11, 12: "And this is the record, that God has given to us eternal life, and this life is in his Son. He that hath the Son hath life; and he that hath not the Son of God hath not life." So that the vital and all important question for everyone of us becomes not am I cultured or uncouth, but am I alive or dead toward God? Have I received God's risen Son who brings me life from above, the life of God, called in the Bible eternal life? Or have I not received Him and am I therefore classed by God as among those who "have not life"?

But how may I receive the Lord Jesus Christ as my Saviour? If I know that, according to Ephesians 2:1, I am "dead in trespasses and sins," as regards my relationship with God; if I believe Jesus Christ gave His life in place of mine, and that now by the receiving of Him as my Saviour I may have eternal salvation, will perceiving these facts in a cold mechanical way give me everlasting life? Most certainly not!

A wealthy man loses all his money, and rather than sacrifice his social position, he agrees to give the hand of his daughter to a rich man whom she despises. At first she refuses point-blank, but when her father shows her the expediency of the marriage, that it is his only hope of being saved from utter want, she consents, and goes through the marriage ceremony, and becomes, according to the law of the land, the rich man's wife. But is her heart really his? Surely not!

36   You see it now, don't you? When a

man and a woman would be truly one, they must love with such a love as to receive each other into those innermost recesses of their hearts in such a deep, true way that they cannot fully express in words all that they feel.

We all have the innermost recess of our beings, which is sacred to us, where emotions stir that no one else could possibly understand. Jesus Christ, God's Son, because of His love for us, claims the right to enter there. He will take no other place in our lives. The love He has shown for us entitles Him to that place. Will I withhold it?

When I think that Christ's love for me was so great that He left His Father's glory and came to earth, becoming truly human that He might suffer and die in my place to give me eternal life, my heart softens toward Him.

If, when I lay sick and helpless in a burning building, a friend had rushed in to save me, and wrapping the blankets about me that I might receive no harm, had himself been critically scarred and burned about the face and arms, would not my heart go out to him? God knows it would.

And now I am face to face with my Saviour. I see Him suffering in the Garden of Gethsemane in anticipation of His death on the cross for me. I see Him in Pilate's Judgment Hall; the soldiers have been striking Him in the face, saying, "Prophesy, who smote thee?" I see them crowning Him with a crown of thorns. They have taken Him bleeding and bruised from judgment to Calvary where they are driving spikes through His hands and His feet. As He is then lifted up to die between two thieves, the people gather around to mock and revile Him, though He· is pouring out His life to redeem them. Then I begin to understand what self-sacrificing love really means as I hear Him cry: "Father, forgive them, for they know not what they do."

But even if we could enter sympathetically into the physical sufferings of Christ until tears streamed down our cheeks, and that was all, we should have failed miserably to comprehend the true significance of the cross.

We read in 2 Corinthians 5:21 that "he (God) hath made him (Christ) to be sin for us, who knew no sin." Come with me, I plead with you, with bowed head and humble heart, and let us, if we may, enter into the soul-sufferings of Christ the Son, and of God the Father, as that Holy One, who loathed sin as we would loathe leprosy, is "made sin for us."

If the higher the development of the physical organism the greater the capacity for pain, then the higher the development of the moral character, the greater the capacity for soul-suffering.

Have you ever heard of a venerable old gentleman, justly proud of his honored name — a man who would sooner lose his right hand than use it to do a dishonorable deed? His son and heir goes astray from the paths of virtue and in a drunken brawl murders someone. And the old man walks no more erect, his head is bowed in shame, and soon his soul-suffering brings his gray hairs in sorrow to the grave.

If that be possible (and it is possible even for us to feel the disgrace of a greater sin than we are used to), think what *sin* must be like in all its awfulness to an absolutely holy God! Now we understand why, in the Garden of Gethsemane, Christ turns in loathing from sin and cries in agony of soul: "My Father, if it be possible, let this cup pass from me; nevertheless not as I will, but as thou wilt" (Matthew 26:39). Yet in spite of that agonized cry from Gethsemane, "God so loved the world that he gave his only begotten Son" to be "made sin" for us, "that whosoever believeth in him should not perish, but have everlasting life" (John 3:16; I Corinthians 5:21).

Now do you understand why I said that if I would retain any ideal of manhood, or any nobleness of character, I dare not reject One who has endured so much for me? My intellect has reasoned it all out; my emotions have been deeply stirred; and now they both appeal to my will for a decision. To be true to my God and myself and my eternal future

I have only one course open, and I must take it. Today Jesus Christ is my personal Saviour and my Lord.

Because of His love to me, because of the way He has blessed me here, and because of my assurance of a glorious hereafter, my heart's desire is that you might share in the blessings I enjoy. *Christ has done all. I say it reverently. He can do no more.* He has borne the penalty of your sin; He has been raised by the power of God; now He presents Himself to you. Will you accept Him as Saviour and Lord?

You are saying: "It seems so mysterious; the mystery of it all baffles me." I do not ask you to understand the mystery of it. I cannot understand its mystery myself, nor can any Christian in this life. I am asking you to rejoice in its fact.

Electricity remains a mystery. We have discovered many of the laws which govern it, but we cannot tell what it really is. You and I do not worry about the mystery of electricity as we make use of its benefits. You must have known men who accepted Jesus Christ as their Saviour and were so changed as to be actually new men in Christ. Will you not let these facts that you have seen for yourself influence you? Yes, it is just as simple as switching on an electric light.

Come, saying: "Oh, God, I cannot understand the mystery of it all. I cannot understand why You cared enough for me to send Jesus Christ to bear the penalty of my sins. But with all my lack of understanding I am willing and I do yield to You; absolutely. I trust in the fact of His death for me and the promise that You have made in John 3:16, 'that whosoever believeth in him shall not perish, but have everlasting life.' "

Just as you leave the mystery of the electric current with the engineer and take the benefits of the light for yourself, so leave the mystery of salvation with God and take the infinite benefits of a personal Saviour to yourself. Yield to Him now — He wants to come into your life. Say and mean it: *"I am Yours, Lord Jesus; yielded to You, body, soul and spirit and You are mine."* Then clinch it by signing the declaration form on the next page.

MY DECISION

Before God, who knows the innermost secrets of my soul, I *accept* Jesus Christ into my life as my Saviour and Lord. I *yield* absolutely to Him. I know, on the authority of His own written Word in John 5:24, that I have everlasting life, for there He says, "Verily, verily, I say unto you, he that heareth my word, and believeth on him that sent me, hath everlasting life, and shall not come into condemnation (judgment); but is passed from death unto life."

Signed ....

Address ....

Date ....

A Further Word:

Perhaps you have not yet made a decision to place your faith in Jesus Christ. Then consider the following:

Someone says, "I am one of those individuals who most emphatically resent being brought to a definite decision on any important subject. It is not that I have no willpower. In fact, I am so strong-willed that I am determined neither to pull up against the current nor pull down with it. I am determined to do nothing but just drift, slowly drift, down the stream of time to——.

"But I hate to think about it! True believers in Jesus Christ look forward to eternity with joy. But I — why am I not honest enough to admit to myself that my resentment at the question is only because I do not want to decide in the way I know I ought to. Yet I must face it some day. Then why not now?"

Now that you have done so, read this little book again. It will seem so much clearer. Then read the entire gospel of John in the New Testament.

Now for the last point, a most important one. If you open your Bible at Romans 10:9 to 11 you will read: "That if thou shalt confess with thy mouth the Lord Jesus, and shalt believe in thine heart that God hath raised him from the dead, thou shalt be saved. For with the heart man believeth unto righteousness; and with the mouth confession is made unto salvation. For the Scripture saith, Whosoever believeth on him shall not be ashamed."

You say you have accepted Christ — go and tell someone — do not be ashamed to confess Him. Why should you be? Suppose I had fallen off the wharf, injuring myself so that I could not swim, and a laborer working on a coal barge had plunged in and saved me. If a month later you saw me walking down Main Street and the same laborer, all begrimed with coal dust, coming up from the opposite direction, and you saw that I noticed him first and deliberately turned to look into a store window so that I would not have to stop and greet him because I was ashamed to be seen talking to him, what would you think of me?

You have declared that you believe the Lord Jesus Christ has given His life to save you. Occasions will arise when you will meet Him face to face in the presence of those who despise Him. Will you be ashamed and look the other way, or will you honor Him in both word and deed as your Lord and Saviour? Having really accepted Him, you must and you will acknowledge Him.

I make no apology for the truth which underlies these pages. I have sought to write what I believe God would have me write in the discharge of my duty to Him and to you. I follow this booklet with the earnest prayer that God will bless it to your eternal welfare.

Yours sincerely,

Robt. A. Laidlaw.

THE SOLDIER'S CHOICE

I was seeking to lead a young soldier to accept the Lord Jesus Christ, but, like most men, he tried to evade the essential issue with the promise, "I'll think it over."

"Harry," I said, "let me illustrate. You are out with the boys some night scouting an enemy post. And on the way back you get hit hard. Another soldier stops long enough to pick you up and carry you back to your own lines, and for his trouble gets two bullets in the back. You are both taken to the hospital and by tender care are won back from the very jaws of death.

"Two months later the doctor brings in a poor fellow who limps badly and moves with evident pain. They stop at your bedside, and the doctor says, 'Harry, I want to introduce you to Bill Smith, the man who risked his life to save you.' You fold your arms and say, 'I'm not sure I want to meet him. I'll think it over.' You wouldn't say that, would you? You would grasp him by the hand and try to tell him something of the gratitude you felt.

"I want to introduce you to the Lord Jesus Christ, the Man who not only risked His life, but sacrificed it, to save you. And you propose to turn your back on Him and say you'll think it over?"

"No," he said, "I'll accept Him." Together we knelt while he told the Lord that he, at that moment, accepted Him as his personal Saviour.

Are you "thinking it over," or have you faced the issue squarely and decided aright?